George and Me

Jamila Gavin

Illustrated by **Briony May Smith**

OXFORD
UNIVERSITY PRESS

The most wonderful time in my life was when my children were young and we were given a beautiful golden Labrador puppy. We loved thinking up a name that would suit her. Because we lived in a valley, and because she was very pale, we all laughed and said she should be called Lily of the Valley. We loved training her, walking her and playing with her, but how embarrassed we were when she stole other people's scones, or burst their beach balls. When, however, in due course, she gave birth to her puppies, how we admired her for being the most loving and caring mother in the world.

I knew that, one day, I would write a story about her. Now why did I choose to call my fictional dog Georgie, and not Lily? Perhaps because my story was fiction not fact. Well, most of it …

Jamila Gavin

Chapter 1
My Biggest Wish

My bedroom window faces east, and when I go to bed, I always leave a gap between the curtains so that the early light of dawn can creep in. Granny gave me a crystal and it hangs straight down between the curtains. When the first rays of the sun strike the crystal, rainbows dance across the ceiling and up the walls. Every morning, I awake and lie looking round my room. If it's a sunny day, the rainbows are dancing. If not, pale grey shadows etch pictures on my ceiling, making strange landscapes or cloud-like animals, and I often see a dog leaping above my head.

I had always wanted a dog. I had gone on and on about it for ages and ages. Though Mum said, 'Maybe,' and Dad said, 'No,' I never gave up. Every birthday and Christmas, I'd have a go – especially if one of my school friends got a pet – and I'd whine, 'Pleeease can we have a dog? Joanie's got a dog, Saul and Nikhil have a dog, Amy's got a dog, and Betsy's mum says they might get a dog one of these days, so why can't we have a dog?' (Betsy is my *best* friend.)

'Because they're dirty, smelly, drooling, demanding, flea-ridden mutts, and they take up space; and someone has to train them, feed them, clean their dishes, shake out their bedding and take them to the vet; and someone has to walk them twice a day, day in, day out, come rain or shine, come blizzard or tornado. Your mother has enough on her plate.'

'So why can't you do it?' I asked.

'Because ... ' Dad spluttered, 'because I hate dogs, and anyway ... Mum and I are going to give you a baby brother instead.'

4

'What?' I gasped. Then, after I'd taken in that piece of information, I said, 'If you don't mind, I'd rather have a dog.' I was remembering Max, Betsy's baby brother, and what a pain he was all the time, always interfering in her life and getting her into trouble if she protested.

But, despite my preference, at dawn one morning, my baby brother was born. I had awoken to the sound of faint kitten-like cries, and when I opened my eyes, rainbows were whirling round my room because it was May, and the sun was up, and the window was slightly open, and a breeze had caused my crystal to spin. Then Granny came into my room.

'Abi,' she whispered, shining like the dawn herself, 'you have a baby brother. Do you want to meet him?'

Granny led me into Mum's room, and there she was, swathed in exhausted happiness, propped up against a throne of pillows like a queen, cradling a bundle.

'Give your little brother a hello kiss,' urged Mum.

So I bent over his screwed-up little face and black downy head, and brushed my lips across his brow. He smelled of milk, and soap, and sunbeams – not that I know what sunbeams smell of – but if they smell of anything, it's probably newborn babies.

'What's his name?' I whispered.

'We haven't chosen one yet,' said Dad, who was smiling fit to burst. 'We thought we'd wait for him to be born and see what kind of person he was.'

I cuddled the baby and snuggled with Mum for a while, and then Dad said, 'Come on, Abi – let's leave Mum now to have a sleep, and we'll go with Granny to her house. Granny thought you should have a special gift on this day – the day of your brother's birth.' He was beaming all over as though Granny's gift was as exciting as the birth of my brother. 'It's waiting for you in her house.'

Granny's house is at the far end of our village. The village is surrounded by soft green hills, and new houses create a fringe around the fields and woods where we love to play after school.

'What is it, Granny?' I begged over and over again, as we walked down the road to her house. 'Is it a present just for me?'

'Just you wait and see,' said Dad mysteriously.

We arrived at Granny's gate and walked up the path. I hopped about impatiently, wondering what the surprise was, as Granny turned the key, pushed open the door and stood for a moment as if listening.

Silence.

'Puppy, puppy, puppy!' Granny's voice coaxed.

Silence.

Not another stuffed dog – I've got five already! I groaned to myself.

Then we heard a little sniffling and scuffling, and a high-pitched 'eek-eek-eeking', and a little, shiny black nose peeped from under a cupboard. Then a furry tumble of golden body wriggled its way out. There, wobbling around on four jellified legs, was a PUPPY!

'AAAAAAAHHHHH! A puppy!' I screamed, and made a rush for it.

'STOP!' ordered Dad. 'You'll frighten her.
Stand back.' And, if you knew my dad, you'd never
have believed what he did next. He fell down on
his knees and crept gently forward, with a doggy
biscuit lying in the palm of his outstretched hand,
whispering, 'Puppy, puppy, puppy! Come on!
Come to Daddy!'

The puppy edged forward, slithering a little on
the floorboards, her nose seeking out the biscuit.

As she swallowed it, Dad scooped up the pup and finally turned triumphantly to face us.

'Meet the new member of the Benjamin family!' he exclaimed. 'She's going to live with Granny until your brother is a little older. Is that OK?'

I was astounded, jubilant, almost speechless, until I gasped, 'Oh yes – *very* OK! Fantastic!' and took her into my arms: a real, live, breathing puppy. 'Thank you, thank you!' I buried my face in her fur.

We found a name for the puppy much quicker than Mum and Dad found a name for my baby brother. Dad's favourite song was called *Georgie Girl*, and as I bent down to cuddle our new puppy, he was whistling it. 'Why don't we call her Georgie?' I cried.

'Hmmm,' murmured Dad, 'I like it,' and he carried on whistling.

I couldn't wait to tell Betsy. As soon as we got back home, I rang her and cried, 'Betsy! I've got a dog, and her name is Georgie!'

A day or two later, they decided on a name for my new brother. They called him Zachary.

Betsy was almost as pleased as I was that we now had a dog. But she moaned enviously, 'I've got a baby brother, and you've got a baby brother, but you've got a puppy too. That's not fair!'

When she came round to see Georgie, she gathered the puppy up in her arms and covered her with kisses, and when she went home, she began to pester her mum. 'Please can we have a dog? Abi's got a dog, Saul's got a dog, Nikhil's got a dog ... '

But Betsy's mum said, 'No. But you can have a rabbit.'

'I don't want a rabbit,' wailed Betsy. 'You can't take a rabbit for walks.'

I said, 'Never mind, Betsy. You can share Georgie with me.'

Granny said that in a few weeks she would take Georgie to puppy-training classes, but in the

meantime, she said we should teach her to sit, stay and lie down. So Betsy and I spent hours in Granny's kitchen training her: Betsy would hold Georgie, saying firmly, 'Sit ... sit ... sit ... ' When Georgie finally sat, I would walk to the far end of the kitchen with a biscuit in my hand. Georgie would keep trying to break loose and make a dash for the biscuit, while I would be saying, 'Stay, Georgie ... stay ... stay ... stay ... ' as I backed further and further away down the kitchen. Then I'd say, 'COME!' and Betsy would let go, and Georgie would hurtle down the room like a cannonball, snatch the biscuit from my hand and wolf it down in one gulp.

Georgie grew stronger each day and bounced about like a beach ball. If anyone came to visit, she raced towards them to say hello, jumping up, pawing at their clothes and nearly knocking them over. And we'd be shouting, 'DOWN, Georgie! DOWN!' At last, though, the training began to work. Soon, we had taught her to sit, stay, come, lie down, and walk to heel.

Georgie was now quite obedient, quite well behaved and not quite so bouncy, and Zac was now a feisty, cheerful baby, and almost as bouncy as Georgie. We didn't call him Zachary any more, but Zac – unless it was to tell him off; then Mum or Dad would say, 'Zachary! NO!'

Mum said training Zac was almost the same as training Georgie.

Chapter 2
Bringing Georgie Home

When Georgie had been living with Granny for nearly a year, we realized that she was getting so big she was becoming too much for Granny to handle. The last straw was when we took Granny out for Sunday lunch and left Georgie behind in her basket, in the kitchen with the door shut – except it *wasn't* properly shut. When we came home, we couldn't believe it: Georgie had chewed Granny's best shoes, nibbled the bottom of the curtain, gnawed away at the wallpaper in the living room, and shredded Granny's library book.

'BAD DOG!' wailed Mum.

'BAD, BAD DOG!' boomed Dad, and Georgie crept away and hid under the table. I went to lie next to her, my arms round her neck. She looked so woebegone.

'Poor Georgie,' I whispered, hugging her to bits. 'Don't worry. I love you.'

'Poor Georgie my foot!' exclaimed Dad. 'I knew

having a dog would be a mistake.' But he didn't mean it. A little later, he stood by the door with the lead in his hand and called out, 'Walkies!' and Georgie was at his side in a flash. I saw Dad smiling and patting her head as he attached the lead to her collar.

'I think it's time Georgie came to live with us now, even if she will cause chaos,' he said.

So, that very day, Georgie moved in with us, along with her dog basket, feeding bowls, chewy toys, dog biscuits and lead.

Betsy and I sometimes took Georgie for walks in the woods on the lead. Everything would be fine until she saw a cat or a squirrel, then she would just rush off like a rocket. The lead would fly from my hand, and I would be left chasing after her crying, 'Georgie – come back! Heel! Stay! Sit! STOP!' I tried every command I knew – but to no avail.

Once, we were walking Georgie through the woods, when suddenly, she saw a squirrel. She lurched forward. I tried to hang on, and Betsy hung on to me, but Georgie was too strong. She tugged the lead, wrenching it from my hand, and tore down the path in full chase. Betsy and I ran after her crying, 'Georgie – come back!' But she wasn't listening. The squirrel sprang up a tree, spiralling higher and higher. Georgie barked and jumped and sprang, leaping up as if she too could follow. What Georgie didn't notice, as she whirled around the trunk barking like a mad thing, was that the squirrel had reached the very top of the tree. Its topmost branches arched across the path and tangled with branches from a tree on the other side. As the squirrel scuttled over our heads to safety, we yelled, splitting our sides with laughter, 'Georgie! You're barking up the wrong tree!'

At first, when Georgie was finally allowed to come and live with us, she had to sleep in the kitchen. But for all our efforts at training – and all the puppy-training classes she had been to – she could be such a naughty dog. Somehow, she wheedled her way into the living room.

Georgie knew she wasn't allowed on the sofa, but she would stand near it looking all innocent, and then, when she thought we weren't looking, she would first shuffle her tummy on, followed by her front legs, and – suddenly – her whole body; and there she was, stretched out on the sofa. Did she think she was invisible?

'GEORGIE, DOWN!' shouted Mum or Dad, or whoever saw her.

'Georgie, DOWN!' repeated Zac, who repeated everything like a little echo these days and Georgie would sheepishly sidle off the sofa and go to her basket. But she continued trying and, despite all our efforts, there she was one day sitting on the sofa next to us, watching the telly.

'She must NEVER, EVER go upstairs,' pronounced Dad, determined that this would be one war he could win, now that he had given in to having a dog, and given in to her sitting on the sofa. 'No dogs on beds!' he declared. 'I draw a line at that!'

But, one night, when Dad was away, and Zac and I had horrible colds, and Mum didn't feel so well herself, Georgie snuck upstairs and got on to my bed.

When Mum found her in the morning, she said, 'Oh, goodness! What will your father say?' I pretended I'd been asleep all along, so never said a word.

Somehow, Dad didn't find out – at least not for a while – and then, when he did, he didn't seem to mind any more, so Georgie always slept on my bed. In fact, the next thing Dad did was buy a camper van, so that we could all go camping at weekends and holidays, and everyone could pile in together – Mum, Dad, Zac, Georgie and me. Sometimes, Betsy came too.

Chapter 3
Betsy, Me and the
Green-eyed Monster

We had always done everything together, Betsy and I, ever since we started nursery. We went to ballet and swimming and gymnastics and drama – not all at once – and when she chose to learn the ukulele, I chose to learn the violin.

'Scritch, scratch, scritch!' exclaimed Betsy with derision. 'We'll all have to get earplugs! Poor Georgie – what agony for her!'

'Georgie joins in!' I declared, and tipped my head back and howled. How we both fell about laughing, because that's what we did! We'd laugh and tease and play silly games, and we went to each other's birthday parties and had sleepovers, and our families joined together to go camping in the summer. So that is why, if anyone asked me, 'Who is your best friend?' I always replied, quick as a flash, 'BETSY!' Even though we had our gang of friends like Amy, Saul, Nikhil and Poppy, Betsy was my best friend.

In fact, because we were always together, the teachers used to mix us up.

Once, Miss Russell said, 'Betsy, it's your violin lesson now,' looking at me. 'You'd better hurry along.'

When Betsy looked up, confused, I said, 'I'm Abi, and I learn the violin. It's Betsy who is learning the ukulele.'

Miss Russell said, 'Oh dear! I'm always muddling you up. Whichever one of you is learning the violin, it's your lesson now.'

I got to my feet while everyone sniggered.

Sometimes, a teacher might say, 'Betsy! Stop that chattering,' but I knew she meant me – as I was the one who was always chattering.

Betsy and I also looked quite alike. Actually, we thought we could be twins: we both had browny skin, black eyes and curly black hair. I was a little taller, she was a little broader, but we both tied up our hair – except at parties, when we were allowed to let it all out like a huge halo, and we felt like pop stars. Our mums often bought us the same T-shirts or fleeces, and we didn't mind a bit if people thought we were sisters.

Then, one day, a new girl joined us. Her name was Nicola – and we were not to call her Nicky! Miss Russell asked Betsy and me if we would look after Nicola until she had found her own feet, so she came to sit at our table in class.

Nicola was as pretty as a princess out of a fairy tale. There was something special about her; a kind of star quality that made everyone want to be her friend. Although Miss Russell thought Nicola needed someone to look after her, I decided very quickly that she seemed quite able to look after herself.

You see, Nicola was like a sun, with planets that orbited around her. All the other children wanted to be her friend. She was famous. Emma's mum had seen her face in a magazine advertising children's clothes. She cut out the advert, and Emma brought it to school. Then Nicola was spotted in a TV advert for a breakfast cereal or something. What a buzz that caused, and we could see even the teachers were impressed.

Being so famous and so beautiful, Nicola could have made friends with anyone in my class, but she decided she wanted to be friends with Betsy. That was the start of my troubles.

It began with Nicola calling for Betsy on her way to school. They both lived on the other side of our village. I was used to getting to school first, as Dad dropped me off on his way to work. I would hop about waiting for Betsy and, when we saw each other, we would race into each other's arms, giggling and exchanging stories. It had been like that for years. But not long after Nicola arrived, I saw Betsy coming into the playground with her – and they were holding hands. Betsy broke away and raced over to me as usual, but Nicola followed. She hooked her arm through Betsy's and said, 'Look! I've something to show you, Betsy,' and pulled her away.

'Betsy!' I called after her. 'Can I see it too?'

Betsy glanced back at me over her shoulder and shrugged, as Nicola continued to drag her off towards a bench. They sat together, side by side, and Nicola reached into her pocket and pulled out an object to show Betsy.

I wandered over, slowly and casually. When I reached them, I said, 'What is it?' But Nicola shoved it back in her pocket, as if it were the most precious object in the universe, saying, 'It's a secret. I'm only showing Betsy.'

I stared at Betsy as if I were looking at a stranger. 'Betsy?' I felt tears coming into my eyes. Betsy jumped up and gave me a hug and said, 'It was just a crystal, a piece of raw amethyst. Nicola's uncle brought it back from Greece. You know, like the ones in the museum.'

'It was supposed to be a secret!' frowned Nicola.

Then the bell rang, so we lined up for the start of the day.

For a while, I thought Betsy and I were – as we always had been – best friends, but it still gave me a pang to see Nicola and Betsy coming to school together, arm in arm. Although we all hung around together for a while, Nicola kept tugging Betsy away and hiding from me, and I knew she wanted Betsy to herself.

Standing in the lunch line, I often told Betsy the next bit of news about Georgie and what mischief she had been getting up to. I knew she wanted to know. She loved Georgie.

'Do you know what Georgie did last night?'

'What?' Betsy asked eagerly.

'Just before bath time, she ran off with Zac's rubber duck. We heard her quacking all over the house. She hid under a bed, but of course we found her because the duck was still quacking in her mouth.'

Betsy laughed and I laughed, and for a moment, I thought everything was all right, but then Nicola came barging in and sat at our lunch table, and only talked to Betsy.

'Betsy! Have you ever ridden a horse?'

'Only on the end of a leading rein in a riding stable,' moaned Betsy. 'I thought it was boring, but I love horses.'

'Then you must come over and meet my pony, Mabel. I've won prizes riding her.'

'What? Do you have your own pony? Oh, lucky thing,' gasped Betsy. 'I've always wanted a pony.'

'More than a dog, Betsy?' I teased.

'Oh, ponies are much more fun than dogs,' retorted Nicola. 'There's nothing like galloping out across a field on a pony.'

'I like both,' said Betsy.

The next day, Nicola joined us, grinning her head off. She grabbed Betsy's arm.

'I've asked Mum, and it's fine for you to come next Saturday to ride my pony, Mabel.' Then she yelled, 'Yippee!' and she and Betsy went galloping away across the playground, leaving me standing there.

That was the first time I ever experienced that horrible feeling in my stomach which wasn't exactly anger, or sorrow – it was different; it was twisting and nauseous; it made the blood flow into my cheeks, then out again till I felt cold; it made me clench my fists and narrow my eyes, and feel as mean as mean could be.

When I got home that night, I snuggled up with Georgie and whispered in her ear, 'I wish Nicola had never come to our school. How I wish the earth would open and swallow her up.'

Only much later did I realize what it was – I was feeling jealous; as jealous as the queen in *Snow White*; as jealous as the ugly sisters in *Cinderella*. Jealousy: the green-eyed monster!

At first, I didn't dream that Betsy would stop being my friend, even if she did like Nicola. But as the weeks went by, I could see that she and Nicola would always come to school together and go home together. Betsy was having more and more sleepovers at Nicola's house – more than she did at mine, or I did at hers.

I kept trying to join in, trying to keep Betsy as my friend. I always had a story to tell about what Georgie had got up to next.

'Hey, Betsy, do you know what Georgie did today?' I cried, running up to her in the playground. And she did listen when I told her how Georgie had found a gap in our hedge, and how she had snuck through to next door's, following the smell of baking scones.

'Mrs Early had left her kitchen door open,' I giggled, 'and Georgie swooped in and scoffed all the scones before you could count to ten.'

Betsy was just beginning to laugh at Georgie's latest escapade, but then Nicola came up and dragged her away.

Betsy nearly always came and walked Georgie with me and Mum after ballet on a Saturday, and then she would stay over for tea. But a Saturday came when Betsy said she wouldn't be walking Georgie with me.

'Sorry, Abi! I'm not coming to ballet this Saturday. Something really exciting is happening. Nicola is being filmed for another TV advert, and she says I can go and watch, and I may even get asked to be in it!'

'Oh!' I said, the jealous feeling rearing up inside me again.

In the playground, I now played with Joanie, Saul, Nikhil and Amy, and my jealousy gave way to a deep sadness. *Was Betsy really no longer my best friend?*

One day, I asked her straight out. 'Betsy, aren't you my friend any more?'

'Of course I am,' she snapped. 'But that doesn't mean I can't be friends with anyone else, does it?' And she ran off to join Nicola.

That day, after school, I crept into Georgie's basket and wrapped my arms round her.

'Oh, Georgie – I don't think Betsy likes me any more, and I don't really know why.'

Georgie grunted with affection and her tail thudded up and down. At least Georgie loved me. Georgie was now my very, very, very best friend.

No one really seemed to notice my sadness except Georgie.

When I asked Mum if I could stay home from school as I wasn't feeling well, she just took my temperature, looked into my eyes and said, 'I think you're OK. Do go, and if you're really not well, I'll get the school to ring me.'

So I went to school. I had now given up trying to be with Betsy, and I joined in with the others instead. But even the others liked to be around Nicola, and I began to feel that they didn't care about me either.

After school, I went straight to Georgie to tell her all about my troubles.

'Miss Russell mixed me up with Betsy again. She told me to stop chattering. But, this time, it wasn't me who was chattering but Betsy, and she and Nicola thought it was very funny that I was the one who got into trouble.' I put my arms round Georgie and pressed my face to her silky ears. 'I don't think anyone likes me any more.'

Georgie looked at me sympathetically.

'Betsy doesn't want to be my friend, Nicola hates me, Saul and Amy and Nikhil and Joanie – they let me play with them, but they always want to play with Nicola. What's wrong with me?'

Georgie sighed, and her tail thumped up and down sadly.

At last, Mum began to notice. 'Where's Betsy these days?' she asked.

'Oh, she's around,' I said in an offhand way. 'But she's best friends with Nicola now.'

Chapter 4
Georgie Becomes a Mum

During the summer, we usually went away on holiday to Spain or France, or sometimes to the seaside in Wales. But this year, the year Zac turned three, Mum said, 'We won't be going on holiday this summer.'

'Why?' I asked.

'Why?' asked Zac.

'Because Georgie is going to have pups!' Mum looked excited.

Dad shrugged his shoulders, saying, 'It's your mother's idea.'

'Puppies?' I squealed. 'Oh, that's amazing!'

'Puppies!' echoed Zac.

'Your mother wanted Georgie to have at least one litter and let her experience the joys of motherhood,' said Dad, looking sour, as though it was all going to be a lot of disruption.

'I think it will make her very happy,' said Mum.

I was thrilled, and jumped up and down at the thought of puppies. I couldn't wait for them to be born. 'Can we keep them?' I asked.

'No,' said Mum. 'I'm going to advertise them right now. They'll all be sold off to good homes – I'll make sure of that.'

'What – ALL of them?' I cried, aghast. 'But Georgie will die of a broken heart if you sell all her puppies.'

'No, she won't. Do you think I'll die of a broken heart when you and Zac grow up and leave home? All creatures leave their mothers and start lives of their own.'

So Mum advertised that Georgie was going to have pups and they were due in July. She said Georgie was a golden Labrador and the father was a black Labrador, and the chances were that she would have some golden and some black puppies.

'The first thing we must do is make a whelping box,' said Mum. It had to be big enough for Georgie to give birth, and lie down safely and comfortably with all her pups. Mum said she might give birth to six or seven, or even more. We had to be prepared.

The space had to have a wooden wall around it, not so high that Georgie couldn't jump out when she wanted to, but not so low that the puppies could get out. At least not till it was safe for them to.

So Mum and Dad got to work and, soon, there was a whelping box in a corner of the kitchen. Mum put Georgie's bed in the box so that she got used to the idea. She jumped in and out as if testing it, then finally settled in her basket in the whelping box. That night, she didn't sleep on my bed.

I was longing to tell Betsy, but I didn't. I hugged Georgie and whispered, 'I won't tell Betsy. She's not my friend any more. But I know she'd love to know you are going to have pups. I bet they'll be beautiful, and if Betsy saw them, she would definitely want one of them. But she won't see them and she won't have one.' I felt so mean, and I expect Georgie thought I was being mean too, because she just gave a deep, groany sigh.

The waiting seemed to last forever. But the day came at last. In the same way as I had been woken to be told of the birth of my brother Zac, Mum came

into my room excitedly and said, 'Georgie's had seven pups!'

'Seven?' I cried, leaping out of bed, and rushed downstairs.

Georgie was lying stretched out in her whelping box. There were seven rat-like creatures, all struggling blindly – because their eyes hadn't opened yet – as they sniffed their way to their mother's milk; three golden puppies and four black ones. Suddenly, Georgie got to her feet and went to a corner of the whelping box.

'Uh-oh! I think there's another one coming,' exclaimed Dad, and sure enough, an eighth puppy – another black one – wriggled out.

'Oh no!' cried Mum. 'Not another one!'

But Georgie didn't seem to mind. She licked the eighth one all over just as lovingly as the others and, closing her great soft jaws over its body, picked it up and carried it over to where its brothers and sisters squirmed and squealed in a writhing heap. Then, amazingly, without squashing any of them, she flopped her huge, golden body down among them and stretched out: the source of life and their well-being.

What a reaction there was from her puppies. They raised their noses, struggling to wriggle their way round in the direction of their mother. The random wriggling turned into a purposeful dash towards her. Blind though they were, they fought fiercely, clambering over each other, their jaws open, bursting with just one single thought – food!

'Oh dear,' I observed, 'there are eight puppies, but there's only room for seven.'

'Yes,' agreed Mum. 'There's going to be a bit of a battle. The last puppy is the weakest and the smallest. We'll have to watch he gets enough to eat.'

But the last pup, small as he was, was as ruthless as the rest. He stuck a paw in one puppy's eye, pummelled his way over another's head, and fought his way to his mother for milk. However, the others were having none of it and, because he was smaller and weaker than the rest, they just trampled all over him.

I was very concerned. 'Hey!' I cried. 'Look! They're not letting that little one get anything to eat.'

'Don't worry. As soon as there's a free place, I'll make sure he gets his share,' said Mum firmly.

Sure enough, one of the bigger pups dropped drowsily away, with a belly full to bursting, then Mum grasped the littlest one and put it in the bigger pup's place. The jaws of the eighth pup opened and soon it was feeding fiercely.

'Hmmm,' murmured Dad. 'That's three things a dog has to learn pretty quickly: one, it's each dog for itself; two, it's survival of the fittest – weaker animals may die; and three, the importance of luck – this one's lucky. It's been born into a good home. If it had been born in the wild, it might have died.'

That first week of our puppies' lives was the first week of the school holidays. It was amazing. I was delirious with happiness; I'd never been so happy. These were going to be the best holidays ever. I forgot all my troubles: I forgot Betsy and Nicola and fretting about school friends; I didn't think about anything else except Georgie and her pups. I didn't

want to go anywhere else. This was better than telly
– just watching the puppies for hours in their dark
paradise of feeding and cuddling, and sleeping and
feeding, and rolling and roughing, and snuffling and
tumbling, and snoozing and snorting; they, in joyful
ignorance, and I, managing to forget that they were
doomed to be torn from their mother's milk and sold
off to different owners, separated forever.

I had already insisted on naming all of them, even
though I knew their new owners would want to give
their own names. There were five girls and three
boys. I called the girls Serena, Florence, Delphine,
Emmelina and Matilda. Zac called the boys Thomas,
Tom, and the littlest and last one Tommy. You see, his
best friend at nursery was called Thomas, and he was
often called Tom and Tommy as well.

By the second week, the puppies' eyes had begun to
open, and they got their first wavery, watery view of
the world; the black and white squares of the kitchen
tiles and the moving shapes that turned out to be the
shoes and hands and looming faces of all of us as we
hovered over them, stroking and making soppy noises.

By the third week, they looked much less like rats. Their mother's milk had begun to have its effect. Their bodies were rounder and plumper, their tummies fatter, their fur had grown fluffy, and their stubby little legs were getting stronger and stronger each day.

Soon, their curiosity outstripped the growth of their bodies, and they began an intense attempt to escape and explore. They were determined to get out of the whelping box. For the moment, their limbs were too feeble to attempt the climb, but Zac and I were allowed to pick up a pup and carry it around for a cuddle, then pop it back in the box again.

Then, one day, Delphine, one of the stronger puppies, was able to reach the top of the whelping box with her front paws by standing on her brother, Thomas. Immediately, another pup saw her as a bridge, and another climbed on her back, and another scrambled over all of them. One by one, they flopped to the floor on the other side.

'Mum!' I yelled. 'The puppies are escaping!'

How we laughed as they clambered on top of each

other, clawing up and up till they were balancing
there on their tummies, seesawing furiously on the
top of the whelping box, before dropping over the
side with a plop on to the kitchen floor.

One after the other, they escaped the whelping
box – all except the last to be born: the smallest
one, which Zac had called Tommy. But Tommy
was going to escape if it killed him. He jumped
and struggled to get over the top, wailing with

frustration as his siblings stumbled joyfully away in all directions to explore. I wanted to lift him out, but Mum said he should learn to do it himself if he was to become as strong as the rest.

'Poor Tommy!' I cried. 'He's desperate to get out. He's so wobbly, and look how they scrambled all over him to get out. I hope he's not hurt.'

'He's fine,' Mum reassured me. 'I'm sure he'll soon get out.'

Tommy knew that if he wanted to discover the joys of the outside world, he must somehow get a head start on the others. So, one day, when Dad had taken Georgie out for a walk, after the puppies had fed and were sleeping one on top of the other in a great furry black and golden ball, grunting in doggy dreams, Tommy wriggled out from beneath them. He heaved himself over their snuffling bodies. What luck! His biggest, fattest sister, Delphine, was pressed up against the wall of the whelping box, and lay there fast asleep and snoring her head off. Being the strongest, Delphine had guzzled the most and slept the longest. Tommy heaved himself on to her back. Delphine groaned and sleepily tried to shake him off, but by this time, Tommy was standing on his two back legs clinging to the top of the box with his claws. Finally awake, Delphine struggled to her feet, but that did Tommy a greater favour, for it raised him even higher and enabled him to get his tummy on to the top. Now there he was – yippee! – balanced on the whelping box wall, seesawing above the vast ocean of black and white tiles on the kitchen floor. He was so excited he nearly toppled back into the box.

'Tommy!' I cried. 'Be careful. Don't fall.' I was longing to help him, but I knew Mum was right when she said he had to learn to do it himself.

With every seesaw, to and fro, Tommy tipped forward ... forward ... further forward ... and ... and ... he toppled over head first, down into free fall over the other side, and hit the kitchen floor with a wallop.

'Tommy!' I screamed, rushing to check he was all right.

'Leave him,' cried Mum, who had also been watching.

'That must have hurt!' I cried.

'But look at him! If it did hurt, he doesn't care,' laughed Mum, and we watched little Tommy quivering with excitement and joy. He had escaped! Freedom!

He staggered forwards. Where was he going? Anywhere – it didn't matter. He was on the move, sometimes sliding on the slippery tiles, sometimes flopping on to his tummy with all four legs splayed out in every direction, before clambering back on to his feet. Nothing was going to stop him. Soon, he had put a considerable distance between him and the whelping box.

Behind him, the other puppies were awake, squealing and peeping. One by one, golden paws and black paws and shiny noses came over the top of the whelping box and with soft plops, fell on to the kitchen floor.

Suddenly, the kitchen door flew open, and Dad came in with Georgie. He stared in amazement at the trail of wriggling puppies staggering across the floor towards him. Waves of strange smells wafted in behind him. The puppies rushed forward even faster towards the Great Outdoors. It was the smell of summer air that assailed their snuffling nostrils; smells carried on the wind, of leaves and trees, cars and petrol fumes, people, cats, and other dogs; smells of dustbins, gardens, newly mown grass and blossoming flowers. It was extraordinary. It was intoxicating. It was terrifying, at least to Tommy, because he was the smallest and feeblest, and he stopped stock still as if he were paralysed with fear. But then his siblings all came belting up behind him and pushed him out of the way in their eagerness to make a dash for the outside world.

Delphine, Tom and Thomas had nearly made it, when Mum screamed, 'Shut the door – they're going to get out!'

'We're going to need a bigger box,' murmured Dad.

It wasn't a bigger whelping box the puppies got –
but the whole kitchen.

For a while, this is how things were: every day,
two or three times a day, and every night, Mum put
layers of newspaper down all across the kitchen
floor. She was weaning them now, and you know
what that means – not just mother's milk any more,
but eight dishes of finely chopped meat and cereal;
and then, you know what that means? Wait for it ...
yes ... MESS! Now the real work began. Poor Mum.

Every night, Georgie and her pups were locked
into the kitchen, and every morning, when Dad
came down to make the tea, we heard him give a
groan as, from the other side of the door, there came
a scampering and scratching of thirty-two little
feet. Taking a deep breath, he would open the door.
Eight puppies, with eight mouths full of little white
sharp teeth, were waiting to pounce. As soon as he
stepped inside the kitchen, the eight sets of sharp
teeth flew at his ankles. They gripped his legs and
clung to his pyjamas as he tiptoed across the floor,
trying desperately to shake off the little beasts.

'Ouch! Oof! Get off!' we could hear Dad
bellowing at them. 'Georgie, can't you keep your
pups in order? Aaaah! When did you say we could
start giving them to their owners?' he yelled.

Chapter 5
Sold Off

In fact, the people who had booked to buy one of Georgie's pups ahead of time were already coming round to see the pups and make their choice, though they wouldn't be able to take them away for at least eight weeks. What cries of delight! What cooings and sighs of heartfelt affection!

'Oh, isn't he adorable!'

'Oh, what a little treasure!'

'She's beautiful.'

'What a champion. I can tell already!'

Soon, they were all accounted for except one. The lady who came last had only one to choose from.

'Oh dear! Is this one mine? I really wanted a golden Labrador.' She picked Tommy up and examined him scrupulously. 'He's not very big. Are his hips all right?'

'Oh yes! He's had the hip test, and he's in perfect health,' my mum reassured the lady.

'And what about this bald spot in front of his left ear?' exclaimed the lady with great distaste. Then she put Tommy down firmly. 'He's not golden, as I wanted. I'm sorry, Mrs Benjamin, I don't think I can take this dog after all. I was hoping for a show dog. I can hardly show a dog with a bald patch.' And she left.

Poor Tommy! How awful to be rejected so young. I picked him up and cuddled him. How mean.

'Just because you're small and have a bald patch, that horrible woman didn't want you. Never mind. We love you, don't we, Georgie?' and I took Tommy to snuggle in next to his mother. 'I think that woman's cruel not wanting Tommy. Looks aren't everything, are they, Mum?'

'No, Abi, they aren't,' agreed Mum. 'Looks are certainly not everything.'

'Well, don't you worry, Tommy,' I muttered fiercely into his little round body. 'I love you. I'll always love you and so will Georgie.' Then I had a thought. 'Mum, if no one wants Tommy, then we'll have to keep him, won't we?' I said with indisputable logic. 'And that would be lovely for Georgie. It must be awful for a mother to lose all her children.'

'Don't start getting ideas again,' muttered Dad. 'We're not keeping Tommy. There simply isn't room for two dogs in this house. We'll just have to re-advertise.'

'But, Dad ... ' I wailed.

'No buts!' said Dad sternly, as he turned on the TV.

'I think Dad's cruel,' I cried.

'Your father's right,' said Mum, a little more gently. 'Even Georgie is a bit big for our household. Two dogs would be impossible.'

'Well, I think you're all mean and horrible,' I shouted, storming into the garden.

'And I think you're mean and horrible too,' echoed Zac, running after me with Georgie following behind, her tail swinging forlornly to and fro. She hated upsets.

'There's at least another three weeks to go before the pups are taken to their new homes. Just enjoy them while you can,' Mum called after us.

Yes, Mum was very firm about that. The puppies must stay with their mother for eight to twelve weeks, even though some of the owners would have taken them straight away. 'That way, they'll get plenty of learning time and lots of good mother's milk.'

When one of the owners begged to have Serena after five weeks because it was for a birthday present, Mum still said, 'No!' very emphatically. Dad thought she was being too particular. Already, he was fed up with getting his ankles nipped by dozens of little teeth every time he walked into the kitchen. But I was pleased. And I still felt there was a chance no one would want Tommy. There was still hope.

I suddenly thought of Betsy. How I missed walking Georgie with her! I wished I could talk to her and share all the fun I was having with the pups. I wondered if she was on holiday somewhere; perhaps she had gone camping with Nicola and her family. We didn't even go swimming with Betsy any more. She didn't know about Georgie and her pups. She didn't know anything about my life, and I didn't know anything about hers. I suddenly missed her; missed having her to chat to and giggle with – and what fun we would have had looking after the puppies together.

I put my arms round Georgie and whispered, 'Betsy would love to see your puppies. I bet she'd want one. I wish she was still my friend.'

Then, one night, five weeks after Georgie had her pups, something awful happened. It all started when Dad was away for a few days on a business trip. Mum had taken us swimming. The puppies were all locked in the kitchen as usual, scuttling about on the newspaper. Although it was summer, it was dark with grey clouds, and it was raining hard that day. Funnily enough, we bumped into Betsy and her mum at the swimming pool, and we stopped to chat.

Betsy's mum said, 'Our Betsy's in an advert on the telly. You must look out for her. She and Nicola are in it together. They look so lovely, the two of them. You must watch. It's the new advert for the Banana Crunch cereal.'

I stared at the girl who had been my best friend. I hadn't seen her for ages, and I missed her all over again. But as her mum chattered to mine about how lovely Betsy and Nicola looked together in some stupid advert, I felt confused and cross again, and I felt the ugly jealousy snake hissing inside my stomach.

Betsy asked, 'How's Georgie? Is she in the car?'

'Oh, no,' I said. 'She's looking after her pups.'

'PUPS?' exclaimed Betsy. 'You mean, Georgie's had pups? Oh, Mum – did you know that? Can we come and see them? Please?'

'Of course,' said my mum. 'We haven't seen you in ages, Betsy. Come any time you like.'

On the way home, I grumbled, 'Why did you ask them to come and see the puppies? Betsy's not my friend any more.'

'Of course she is,' said Mum. 'But all friends have blips – it's part of growing up. Just you see, once she's got over the glamour of Nicola, she'll be back to being your friend. I'm sure of it. Oh dear! We've been out a long time. I hope the pups haven't got up to any mischief. They'll be starving!'

It was still raining when we rushed inside with all our wet swimming things. We braced ourselves outside the kitchen door. We could hear scampering and whimpering and scuttling about. We knew the puppies must have drained every last drop of milk from Georgie and were now desperate for their solid food. Mum opened the door. The puppies made a dash for our ankles and we felt their sharp little teeth dig into our legs. The newspaper Mum had scattered across the floor was chewed to bits. Georgie was pacing up and down, but her tail began to wag furiously at the sight of us. 'Thank goodness you've come back at last,' she seemed to be saying.

'Ow, ow!' I laughed. 'Their teeth are like needles. Ow! That hurt!'

'Grr ... Grr ... ' Zac growled playfully at them, and picked up three wriggling pups at a time.

Some of them dashed back to Georgie for more milk, but now she was irritable and, to my amazement, swiped them away.

'Oh dear! Everyone's hungry and cross,' cried Mum, throwing down the swimming bags and hurrying towards the kitchen cupboards. 'I'll just put out the food for the puppies then see to you two.'

'I'm starving!' I moaned, and headed for the biscuit jar.

'I'm starving,' cried Zac. 'Bicky, bicky!'

'No! No! Don't snack!' begged Mum. 'Here, Abi! Put a portion of this meat into each bowl and then a teaspoon of vitamin oil. If you feed the puppies, I can get on with feeding you.'

In the middle of this scramble to get food into all our empty tummies, the doorbell rang sharply, twice. *Ding-dong! Ding-dong!*

'Who can that be, at this time?' Mum sighed in a harassed voice, and reluctantly put down the tin of baked beans she was just about to open for us.

I had filled eight bowls with mince and vitamins for the puppies, but I waited before putting them down on the floor. *Who could be at the door?* I wondered.

The pups squealed and fretted with impatience.

'Feed them, feed them,' cried Mum as she went to answer the door. 'Yes?'

I could tell by her voice that she was speaking to strangers.

'We've come about the pups you advertised,' said a man's voice – young, but assertive. 'Labs, isn't it?'

'Er ... yes.' Mum sounded uncertain. 'Yes, we have Labrador puppies, but they are all sold, except for one.'

'So you have one left, do you?' a young woman's voice asked eagerly, as she pushed forward through the front door and into the hallway, before peering into the kitchen.

'Well! If you've got one left, we'll have it then,' said the young man's voice. 'I've got the money right here in my pocket.' He pulled out a wodge of notes. They took the liberty of stepping further inside the kitchen, and looking at Georgie and all the pups gobbling up their food.

'Oh, but ... you can't just have him like that ... ' stammered Mum.

'Why not? You want to sell your pup, don't you? And we want to buy one. We have the money right here, so what's the problem?'

Zac and I crowded up curiously behind Mum. Who were these people? I didn't like them at all.

'Well, in the first place, I don't know you,' Mum said, trying to be forthright. 'I don't know where or how you live, and I have to make sure that my puppies go to suitable homes. In the second place, it's far too early yet to let any of the puppies go. They are only five weeks old, and I want them to stay with their mother until they are at least eight or even twelve weeks old. So I think it's best if you come back another time and we can discuss it.'

The young man advanced another step into the kitchen and Mum fell back a step, looking disconcerted.

'I'm Mike and this is Beverley, my girlfriend.'

Mum nodded, 'Hello, Mike and Beverley.'

'I can understand your concern,' he said, 'but, look – I'm a farmer. I have a farm in Lower Marley. I was brought up with animals. I know all about them. We've had dogs and pups all our lives. If I was just someone looking for a pet, I'd agree with your point of view all the way, believe me. But I want to train my pup my way, and now's the age to start. If you let me take the pup, she'd be fine, really.'

'He ... ' interrupted Mum in a flat voice.

'*He*, is it? Oh, that's all right,' exclaimed the young woman. 'Males are better guard dogs, aren't they?' Her voice trailed off and she looked uneasily at the man.

'Please, Mrs ... er ... '

'Benjamin,' murmured Mum.

'Please, Mrs Benjamin.' The young man continued his plea after returning his companion's glance with an expression which could have been interpreted as a silent, *Shut up. Leave this to me.* 'You see, we've been hunting everywhere for a black Lab, and we were just on our way home when we realized from the advertisement that we were quite close to you. So we called in on the off-chance. Like I said, we're from Lower Marley and it would be so convenient if we could just take the puppy home with us now. There's so much work on a farm, and it would be difficult for us to come again. Where we live is ideal for a dog. Being a farm, there's plenty of space. He'd be out all day, having tons of exercise, and you know how much exercise these Labs need!'

The young man looked at Mum intently with beseeching blue eyes. They were his strongest point. He knew how to use them, looking her straight in the eye and giving an impression of honest common sense and understanding.

'They're still too young to be outside for any length of time,' said Mum. 'They mustn't go for walks for at least another five weeks, and they need full-time care.'

'I know, I know! Look here – I was brought up with dogs, Mrs Benjamin. I've looked after newborn puppies. I know exactly what they need.

I once had to hand-rear seven puppies. They all lived,' he said with easy confidence.

'Well ... ' Mum hesitated. She looked at me. 'I only want to do what's best for them ... ' Her voice trailed away.

'Mum!' I wailed in horror as I saw she was wavering. I rushed over to Tommy and picked him up, holding him fiercely to my chest.

'Mum, you can't let him go. He's too young!'

'You can't let him go, Mum!' echoed Zac.

'Oh, so this is the little puppy, is it?' The young woman spoke again. She came over to me and stroked Tommy's head. 'He's adorable!' she enthused. 'Can I hold him?'

I backed away. 'Anyway, this one's bald,' I announced possessively, swinging Tommy away from the woman's touch. 'You'd never be able to show him.'

'It's only a little bald spot. Anyway, we don't want a dog for showing, we want a farm dog. Looks don't matter that much. Labs are working dogs, aren't they? And Mike can take him hunting. After all, they are hunting dogs too, aren't they, Mike?'

'Hunting?' I was horrified.

'Mike likes his hunting,' smiled the young woman. 'That's what we're looking for.' She turned back to me. 'Go on, let me hold him.'

I stood frozen while she gripped Tommy's body. I noticed her long red fingernails and bright lipstick; I noticed her skin-tight jeans, silky blouse and high-heeled shoes. She didn't look at all like a farm person.

I held on to Tommy. I didn't want to let him go. He began to squirm and Georgie began to growl as if she agreed with us. She had leaped out of her whelping box, and her nostrils were drawn back menacingly. Tommy wriggled and squealed plaintively, as if he knew his whole future was on the line. Georgie crouched down on her haunches like a lion ready to pounce, growling deeply in her throat.

Mum grabbed her collar. 'No, Georgie.'

Georgie began barking, frantically trying to pull away from Mum's grip. She was desperate to spring into defence of her pup.

'Oh dear – I'll have to shut her away,' murmured Mum, and she pushed Georgie into the utility room and shut the door. Georgie went mad with howling, and scratched loudly from behind the door.

I felt sick inside. I hugged Tommy even tighter to me, but the woman gripped his body, and I was afraid that poor Tommy would be torn apart in this battle of wills, so I let go.

'Oh, he's a darling!' the young woman enthused, pressing her face into Tommy's fur. 'That little bald spot doesn't matter one teeny-weeny little bit.

Anyway, I expect it'll grow over as he gets older.'

'So, is that settled then?' demanded the young man. He flicked through the wad of notes in his hand and proceeded to count them out in tens on the kitchen table. 'That right?' He patted the money – a done deal.

'Mum, no!' Zac – my little brother – stepped forward, bold as a warrior. 'Don't take Tommy!'

'He's too young. You said so yourself,' I argued.

'He's too young!' echoed Zac.

'The pups have to stay with us for eight or even twelve weeks. That's what you said, Mum! You can't let him go,' I urged.

'You can't let him go!' cried Zac desperately.

'I know, Zac,' Mum sighed with exhaustion. 'But … ' I could see she was struggling to justify her weakening stand. 'But … Tommy is the only one who hasn't yet got a home, and you know we can't keep him. If these people are farmers and know all about looking after animals, then maybe I'd be wrong not to let them have him. Most of the people who've come wanting to buy either live in the town, or want show dogs. Mike and Beverley sound ideal.'

Outside, the rain was now lashing at the windows, and the pups were scampering about.

'I wish Dad was here,' I muttered angrily. 'He wouldn't let Tommy go.'

'I'm not so sure,' answered Mum wearily. 'He was very keen to know all the pups were sold.'

'Look!' the young man said, as if struck by a bright idea. 'Here's our name, address and telephone number.' He took out a scrap of envelope from his pocket and scribbled on it. 'You can come and visit us, or telephone, any time you want to know how the puppy's getting on. He'll be all right, I promise you. We love animals. Other people may be more picky than us. They may not like a weak, little thing like this, or one with a bald patch. You may not find others like us who would give him as good a home as we can. I mean, it's a farm! What could be better?'

Mum suddenly gave way. 'I suppose if you are so experienced with animals, he'll be in good hands,' she reasoned, as if trying to reassure herself. 'Abi, Zac! Give Tommy a last cuddle while I look for a good cardboard box for him.'

I almost snatched Tommy back from that woman's hands. Even though Mum and Dad had made it quite clear we couldn't keep Tommy, I couldn't bear to see him go – and especially not to these strangers who had come into our house on this dark, rainy evening. I had still thought if no one wanted Tommy, we might have been able to keep him. But now he was going, and I couldn't stop it. I snuggled my face into his fur, and Zac embraced us both.

'This is wrong,' I whispered into Tommy's fur.

Mum found a cardboard box, lined it with newspapers and popped in a couple of Tommy's rubber toys.

'He's just eaten, so he should be all right for the next two hours or so. Here's a bottle of vitamin oil to add to his food. You need to feed him every two to three hours. You can do that, can you? He needs someone who's in all day.'

'Don't worry!' the woman reassured us. 'I'm in all day. I'll look after this pup like he's my baby,' and she cuddled Tommy, murmuring in his ear.

Mum wrote out a feeding chart for the couple, which told them the time of each meal and what they should give Tommy to eat.

'Right then! Best be off,' said the man.

The woman came and extricated Tommy from my arms. He looked bewildered.

'Goodbye, Tommy,' I wept. 'I hope you have a wonderful life.'

'Goodbye, Tommy. Have a wonderful life,' said Zac solemnly.

'Cheerio then!' the couple said, and they were gone.

We saw the money on the table. Mum didn't touch it.

Georgie was clawing and whining at the utility room door. Mum let her out. Georgie rushed over to the front door, as if she wanted to chase after them and get back her baby.

'Oh, Mum!' I wept. 'Look at Georgie! You've broken her heart!' Then I glanced at Mum. There were tears in her eyes and her face was stricken with remorse.

Tommy was the last to be born, and the first to leave home. But it wasn't just that he had gone too soon; there was something about the man and woman I didn't like and didn't trust. If they wanted a working and hunting dog, why would they take Tommy who was the smallest and weakest pup? I knelt down to comfort Georgie.

'Oh, Georgie – I'm so sorry. It must be awful to have your puppy wrenched away into the hands of strangers.'

Georgie's tail thudded slowly and sadly.

By the time we had eaten and finally trooped morosely off to bed, the money for Tommy was still untouched on the table.

Chapter 6
Remorse

All night long, I tossed and turned, thinking about Tommy – how he must be crying for his mother, and how he was with that strange couple whom I didn't like. If they really loved dogs, how could they have taken Tommy away from his mother too soon? I heard the wind and rain lashing outside. I wondered where he was; where was he sleeping? Not snuggled up against Georgie, that's for sure. When I finally fell asleep, I dreamed of poor little Tommy crouched in his cardboard box, quivering with misery, his eyes straining in the darkness, and his ears listening with intense curiosity and fear to the strange sounds and smells in an alien place. He wanted to get out. He began to scratch and struggle, and he forced strange, barky squeaks from his throat because he hadn't yet learned to bark properly. I awoke with a cry. 'No!'

The next morning, I pestered Mum with questions.

'Do you think Tommy's all right? Do you think he slept in that cardboard box all night? Have they remembered to feed him?'

'I don't know, Abi. I'm sure he's all right.'

'Phone them up! Ask what kind of night he had. Please, Mum,' I begged.

Mum agreed; she found the phone number and rang it. There was no answer, so she left a message.

'Sorry to bother you,' she apologized. 'My children just wanted to know how the pup got on last night – it's the first time he's been away from his mother.' She asked for a quick call back, but none came that day, or the next.

Meanwhile, Georgie missed her eighth pup. She hunted for him all round the house, and when she was let outside, she hunted for him all round the garden. Finally, she went to the front gate, looking up and down the road in the hope that he would return.

The rain eventually stopped, and it was a beautiful, glistening, sunny day when Betsy and her mum turned up to see the pups. Seeing them come in felt like the good old days.

Of course, there were shrieks of delight as Betsy and her mum fussed over Georgie, and gathered the puppies up to cuddle, and asked what their names were and how long they were staying before being taken to their new homes.

'Oh, Mum!' wailed Betsy. 'Can't we have one of Georgie's pups?'

'I can't cope with a dog. Sorry, Betsy,' said her mum firmly. 'You know what they say: a dog is for life. Having a dog is like having a baby. They have to be looked after and cared for.'

'I'd do that,' cried Betsy.

'Anyway,' I said sadly, 'all of Georgie's pups have been sold.'

'Oh!' Betsy looked disappointed.

'Thank goodness!' Betsy's mum winked at mine.

'You haven't been round recently to walk Georgie,' my mum said gently to Betsy. 'We always love to see you – and so does Georgie.'

'Where's she got to?' asked Betsy, looking around the kitchen.

'She's probably gone to sit at the front gate. We let one of her pups go to a new owner, and she's been looking for it ever since.'

'Oh, how sad!' cried Betsy's mum. 'A bit early to leave its mother, I suppose.'

'I know,' wailed my mum. 'I feel like a criminal. I wish I hadn't given in.'

We all looked so woebegone that Betsy's mum said, 'Why don't we take Georgie for a walk in the woods? Can we?'

'That's a great idea,' Mum brightened. 'We all need cheering up – and so does Georgie.'

Because it had rained the previous night, we put on our wellies and jackets. Mum took Georgie's lead off the hook and then we went out to the gate calling, 'Georgie, walkies!' But Georgie wasn't there.

'Georgie?' called Mum.

'Georgie!' I called, and so did Zac, and Betsy, and her mum. But no Georgie appeared. We rushed all round the house and all round the garden, yelling our heads off. 'Georgie! Georgie!' But there was no Georgie.

'She must have got out!' exclaimed Mum in horror.

'She's gone looking for Tommy,' I marvelled.

'She's looking for Tommy,' agreed Zac.

'She must have jumped the gate,' cried Betsy's mum with awe.

'Which way would she have gone?' I asked in panic. 'We must go and find her.'

I knew what it was like to feel jealousy slithering in my stomach; now, I felt fear. Fear tumbled round my stomach; I felt sick, I felt numb. I wanted to cry, but I had no tears. I wanted to rush off and look for Georgie, but my body felt paralysed. A storm of questions whirled round my brain: *Where was Georgie? How could she possibly know where to go to find her puppy? What could we do? Where could we go?*

'Where did you say Tommy's new owners lived?' asked Betsy's mum.

'Lower Marley,' answered my mum gloomily. 'I'd better ring them in case Georgie turns up.'

She rang. But again, there was no answer, and she left another message.

'I think we should go and look for her ourselves. We'll walk along the road to Lower Marley – the road they would have driven away on.'

Mum quickly phoned Granny and begged her to come round and take care of the pups while we all went searching for Georgie. Then Betsy's mum, my mum and Zac strode off down the road, and Betsy and I followed behind.

At first, Betsy and I walked in silence, then after a while, Betsy told me they had just had a week on a farm in Wales, where there were at least three dogs.

'They were sheep dogs, and you should have seen the way they rounded up the sheep! They're amazing. The farmer taught me to whistle. Do you remember how we trained Georgie with words like sit, walk, come and stay? Well, the farmer has a whole set of whistles which make the dogs do what he wants.' Betsy put two fingers in her mouth and let out a piercing whistle.

'Wow, Betsy!' I was so impressed, and I tried too – but nothing happened.

Suddenly, we heard a frantic barking. Everyone stopped.

'Is that Georgie?' asked Betsy's mum.

I said, 'Betsy, whistle again,' so Betsy whistled again. Again, a dog barked and barked somewhere off the road, in the woods. We all charged into the undergrowth yelling, 'Georgie, Georgie!'

There was a crashing, a whining and a barking as finally, emerging through the trees, we saw a very bedraggled Georgie. She hurtled towards us, and flung herself upon me, then upon Zac, and then Mum, and then back to me.

I clasped her in my arms. 'Georgie! You gave us such a fright, running away like that.'

'She didn't run away,' corrected Zac. 'She went to look for Tommy.'

'Well, let's go home now and make a few more telephone calls to try and find out how Tommy is doing,' said Mum. 'Come on, everybody.'

But Georgie wasn't having that. Oh no – there was only one thing on her mind: to find her puppy. She ran back into the woods.

'Georgie, come!' commanded Mum again. But Georgie didn't come. Instead, she stopped and made strange whining noises in her throat before continuing deeper into the woods.

Betsy tried to whistle again, but it was the wrong type of whistle.

'Oh dear, I don't think I know the right one to make her obey,' said Betsy.

'But you found her for us, Betsy!' I cried joyfully. 'Come on – she wants us to follow.' I plunged into the undergrowth.

Georgie stopped again, looking at us and whining. Then she backed away and ran deeper into the woods. Just before she was out of sight, she stopped again.

'Abi's right. Georgie wants us to follow her,' said Betsy's mum.

'Follow, follow,' chanted Zac.

'Then we'd better follow,' said Mum.

So we all followed. Georgie led us on and on till we came to a fence. Over the fence was farmland with cattle grazing. Georgie ran alongside the fence, and we followed her. She crawled under a stile, and we climbed over. On across an empty field she ran, and into another field and through another stile, and we followed too.

'Is this the way to Lower Marley?' Mum wondered. 'Or are we getting well and truly lost? Zac's going to get tired. We can't go on much further. Let's go home. We can get the car and drive to Lower Marley.'

'We can't give up now!' I cried insistently.

'Can't give up now,' echoed Zac.

Chapter 7
Searching for Tommy

Georgie kept moving ahead of us, stopping every now and then to check that we were following her. But where was she leading us?

We came to another field, and another stile. Georgie crept under it, we climbed over it, and there, on the far side of a rippling barley field, we saw a small red-brick cottage, and beyond it, a few farm buildings.

Georgie was moving more quickly now, and we, too, broke into a run. She went through the barley field; we went round it. We saw a five-bar gate. Georgie had vanished through the hedgerow. We opened the gate and went through into a farmyard. Somewhere beyond, we heard Georgie barking her head off. We raced along a track and found ourselves at the red-brick cottage, and there she was, leaping up at the front window. We clustered round her and looked inside.

'Oh, my goodness! It's Tommy! Georgie's found her puppy!' cried Mum.

While I pushed my face up to the window, Mum knocked on the door.

We all waited, suddenly anxious, looking at each other and wondering what we were going to say. But no one came to the door. Mum knocked again – louder. Nothing. We looked through the kitchen window, and what a mess we saw: the sink was full of unwashed dishes; there was a table cluttered with papers and dirty plates; and there, running round and round in circles, was Tommy. His food bowl was empty, and his only bed was the cardboard box Mum had given the couple to take him away. Georgie barked frantically. Inside, Tommy heard her and began desperately trying to leap up on to the windowsill.

'Poor Tommy!' I wailed. 'Look! He's all by himself. Mum! How can we get him back?'

At that moment, we heard a tractor clunking into the yard. The engine stopped. A man appeared, striding down the path towards us. He looked puzzled, and not very pleased at the sight of Georgie, who was barking and leaping around.

'Can I help you?' he asked gruffly. He had a stern, weather-beaten face, with grey whiskers and grey hair flopping beneath a tweedy flat cap. 'Put that dog on a lead, if you don't mind. This is a working farm here.'

Mum apologized profusely and, thank goodness, Georgie didn't fuss when Mum attached the lead to her collar, though she whined and growled.

'We're looking for the couple who live in this cottage. I believe they work on your farm?'

'Oh no!' said the farmer. 'I just rent this cottage. If you mean Bev and Mike, the two of them have jobs in the town.'

'You mean they are away all day – both of them?'

'Yup! She works at the newsagent, and he's a manager at the electronics factory.'

'Mum!' I exclaimed, horrified. 'That means no one is feeding Tommy every two hours; no one's there to cuddle him and play with him. Poor Tommy!' I was nearly crying.

Mum looked aghast. 'I should have known there was something wrong. I believed them when they told me they were farmers and that someone would always be home to take care of the puppy.'

'Well, this is a right old pickle,' said the farmer grumpily, and not at all pleased. 'I don't like trouble. I told them fair and square when they came that they weren't to have any pets – least of all a dog. I have a Jack Russell, see? And he doesn't like other dogs on his patch.'

'Please! Please help me to get the puppy back,' begged Mum.

'Please,' we all wailed in unison.

'You are my only hope,' pleaded Mum. 'I have no legal right to take him back, because I sold him fair and square. They paid me what I asked for. But if you say that they shouldn't have brought the puppy on to your farm without your permission, then you are the only one who can take proper action.'

'Well, Missus, I'll have a word with them when they get in from work. But I can't guarantee anything. It's their dog, but my cottage. They'll have to make a choice: give you back the pup or leave my cottage.'

Chapter 8
The Long Wait

Mum and the farmer exchanged phone numbers, and we all set off back across the fields.

'They're awful,' I cried. 'I always thought they were lying about being farmers!'

'It's all my fault,' groaned Mum. 'I just thought no one would want to buy him, being so small, and with a bald patch. And we can't cope with two dogs.'

'We could have him, couldn't we, Mum?' cried Betsy.

'Well ... I don't know ... '

'Oh yes – please! If we get him back – please have him,' I cried passionately. 'It would be like keeping Tommy in the family, and Georgie would be so happy.'

'Then Abi and I can train him, just as we trained Georgie!'

'Betsy, no! Don't go on about it,' said her mum.

'Anyway, we may not get him back,' murmured Mum gloomily. 'I don't really know why they wanted him in the first place. But who can read other people's minds? All we can do is wait and see. We may hear by tonight.'

So we made our way back home, feeling a little hopeful, but not much. This time, Georgie plodded along, not attempting to drag us back to Tommy. It was as if she knew that, having found her lost puppy, she must now get back to the others.

Betsy took over holding Georgie on the lead, and it was just like old times. Yet we didn't talk about being friends or not being friends.

'I saw you on the telly,' I said.

'Did you?' Betsy looked pleased. 'It was such good fun. They want me to do some more.'

'Wow!' I said. 'You'll become a celebrity! I'll have to ask for your autograph.'

'Oh, don't be silly,' laughed Betsy. 'But the funny thing is, they've asked me to do another, but they haven't asked Nicola. Isn't that a shame?'

I shrugged, but inside my stomach, the green-eyed monster whispered, *Good*.

We reached the woods, and Mum called out to let Georgie off the lead now so that she could have a good scamper around. Ahead of us was an agonizing wait to know what Tommy's fate would be.

Betsy and her mum peeled off at the road to go to their house.

'You will give us a ring and let us know what happens, won't you?' cried Betsy's mum.

When we got home, Granny made some tea for us all while Mum told her everything that had happened. We surveyed Georgie and her pups.

They were rolling all over her, having little snacks and chasing their tails.

'Who would have thought these little creatures could bring such joy, and such anxiety?' said Granny.

We didn't talk much through tea. We were all worrying about Tommy. Even Georgie, who would normally have sat near the table, her jaws drooling with longing for our sandwiches and crisps, sat on her haunches in the whelping box looking like a melancholic sphinx.

It was almost bedtime when the phone rang. We all stopped like statues. Mum answered it. She listened. We looked, our eyes questioning, becoming more and more frantic. She put the phone down.

'Farmer Horton wants me to drive over now, if I can. They're back from work, and he thinks I need to speak to them.' She looked at Granny. 'Can you stay on a bit?'

'Of course,' said Granny.

'Please, Mum, can I go with you?' I begged her.

Mum hesitated, but gave in. 'All right,' she said.

I noticed her scoop up the money still lying on the table where the couple had left it to pay for Tommy.

Zac opened his mouth, but – before he could say, 'Me too!' – Granny leaped in and said, 'Zac, let's give Georgie a good clean up after her escapades in the woods and fields.'

Mum and I hurried off before he could change his mind.

We drove into the farmyard and parked next to the tractor. There was another old car parked there as well. We walked along the track to the red-brick cottage. Tommy was in that cottage, and my heart was in my mouth.

'Here goes,' murmured Mum, and knocked on the door.

It opened. There was the man, Mike.

Mike looked defensive. 'So – you came checking on me, did you?' he said to my mum.

'I rang and left messages,' said Mum. 'But you never returned my calls. You knew I was anxious about the pup. And guess what? It was his mother, our dog Georgie, who ran away to find her pup, and we followed her. Goodness knows how she knew where to find you. Now that's love. That's mothering. All this stuff about being home all day to care for the pup and feed him every two hours, and how you were brought up with dogs and lived on a farm – all lies, wasn't it? You've both been out since half past eight this morning, haven't you?' Mum was cool as a cucumber. 'This puppy has been kept a prisoner without proper feeding or fresh air for the last eight or nine hours. That's cruelty.'

At that moment, Beverley came out. She was holding Tommy.

'Here, take him back,' she said. There were tears in her eyes, and I suddenly felt a little sorry for her. 'It's because it's my birthday soon, and when Mike asked me what I wanted as a present, I said a dog – the kind I can take walking and he can take hunting. We had seen your advertisement and we were nearby, so Mike said, "Let's get it now." I didn't think he would take me seriously. But that's Mike all over – generous, impulsive. "If you want a dog, you shall have a dog." But he wanted it now. He didn't think it through. I didn't think it through.'

'Hey, Bev!' Mike protested. 'Don't give it back. It's yours. I paid for it good and proper.' He looked as if he would try and wrench Tommy from her arms.

At that moment, Farmer Horton strode up.

'You can't have a dog on my farm,' he said categorically. 'I told you that when you came. The choice is yours. Give the dog back, or leave this cottage immediately. I've got a Jack Russell, and I tell you now, he'd have that pup for dinner. I'm not having any trouble trying to keep them apart. So you'd better make up your mind.'

'I've brought back your money,' said Mum, gently holding it out.

'Here!' Beverley handed me the pup, and Mum put the cash in Mike's hand.

'That's settled then,' said Farmer Horton stiffly, and walked away.

'Thank you,' said Mum softly to Beverley. 'I blame myself for what happened. I should have known better, and for that, I'm sorry. I promise you that if you love dogs, this is for the best.'

Then Mum herded me back to the car and, I can tell you, I held Tommy so close, a team of wild horses would not have taken him away from me.

Chapter 9
Friends

We brought Tommy into the house and placed him before a joyful Georgie. She sniffed him from top to toe, checking that it was really her puppy. Then she licked him all over for good measure.

Dad came back from his trip away to find merry chaos, with the puppies tumbling about with gusto. At the sight of him, they hurtled forwards, nipping at his ankles, chewing his shoes and wrestling with his legs. Dad beamed, and Georgie barked her head off.

'Hey, hey! Get off! They're my best trousers!' Dad tried to shake away the nipping puppies.

'Best trousers!' shouted Zac, leaping on to Dad.

'Hey, you!' cried Dad, lifting him up into his arms. 'You're as bad as the pups. Now, what have you been up to while I was away? What's all this fun I see? What's been going on?'

We looked at each other and burst out laughing. Then Mum told him the whole story. I wasn't sure if Dad was pleased or not to hear of the efforts we had all gone to in order to get Tommy back.

'Hmmm!' Dad snorted. 'But he still has to go.'

The next morning, Betsy, Max and their mum came round. They were longing to see Tommy reunited with Georgie, and his brothers Thomas and Tom. While our two mums sat sipping tea, we played with the pups. But it was Betsy who cuddled Tommy and didn't want to put him down.

I whispered in Georgie's ear, 'I think Betsy loves Tommy. I wish she could have him, then at least one of your pups would be nearby.'

The summer holidays ended. We went back to school. Once more, Dad dropped me off early and I waited in the playground for my friends to arrive. I saw Betsy. I suddenly felt anxious. Would she still be my friend, now that we were back at school? She walked in alone with her mum, not with Nicola. In fact, Nicola was walking arm in arm with another girl. When Betsy saw me, she came rushing over – just as she used to. We hugged and giggled. Betsy asked about Georgie and her pups, and I told her that, one by one, the owners had been coming to collect their puppies.

'Poor Georgie,' sighed Betsy. 'Fancy losing your babies like that.'

'I know,' I sighed, 'but maybe it's just as well the puppies are beginning to go. They're getting really pushy and boisterous, and always trying to feed from Georgie's dish. If anything makes Georgie mad,' I said, 'it's a pup trying to steal her food. She growls, and with one swipe of her paw sends it skidding across the kitchen.'

'And Tommy?' asked Betsy wistfully. 'Has he got an owner yet?'

'Not yet!' I replied. 'No one seems to want a small, scruffy puppy with a bald patch. But my mum says, can you come home after school today for tea, so you can play with them? She's checked with your mum.'

'Yeah! And we can do some more puppy-training,' cried Betsy.

When we got home after school, Tommy was the first to come to the door to greet us. My

goodness, he looked handsome. He stood half
in and half outside; the sun falling down on him
like a spotlight. He looked so sleek and shiny black.
Although he had been the smallest, he was now
taller, and more muscular, and ready for anything.

'We're going to start training Tommy!' I told Mum.

So while Mum made tea, I held Tommy, and
Betsy backed away down the kitchen with a biscuit
in her hand. 'Stay ... stay ... stay ... COME!'

I let go of Tommy, and he hurtled down the
kitchen and wolfed down the biscuit in one gulp.

Towards the end of the evening, there was a knock on the door. It was Betsy's mum, come to collect her. I opened the door to let her in. She looked at me very seriously but with a twinkle in her eye, and said, 'I've come about the puppy. You know, the small, black one with the bald patch. If he's still available, I'd like to have him.'

The house must have shuddered with our cries of joy. I thought Betsy would go berserk with happiness.

It was the best of all possible outcomes: the puppy would have a loving home; Georgie could see Tommy almost any time she wanted; and I could go on helping Betsy to train Tommy, just as she had helped me to train Georgie.

Finally, after Betsy and her mum had left with Tommy firmly snuggled into Betsy's arms, I crept to Georgie's basket in which she had spread out her full length. She looked thoroughly pleased to have all the space to herself at last, and I whispered in her ear, 'Georgie, do you know the really, really good thing? Betsy and I are best friends again.'

* * *

These days, I wake up in the morning, and still find it hard to believe that this heavy, slumbering lump across my feet is a dog – my dog Georgie – and that it was *my dad*, the one who said he never wanted a dog in the house, who got her for me.

A protesting groan comes from deep inside Georgie as she feels me shift in my bed. She's not ready for the day to begin. I can hear my younger brother Zac singing to himself until it's time to get up. I lie quietly, watching the dawn sunshine catch Granny's crystal hanging there in my bedroom window between the curtains, turning the light into rainbows. They thread their way across the ceiling and gently dance. I know that in a few moments, Georgie will wake up and bound downstairs to the door. 'Walkies!' she'll bark, and the whole house will leap into life.